NOW DO YOU KNOW WHERE YOU ARE

NOW DO YOU KNOW
WHERE YOU ARE

DANA LEVIN

Copper Canyon Press
Port Townsend, Washington

Cover art: Johannes Janssonius, *Tabula Anemographica seu Pyxis Nautica Ventorum Nomina Sex Linguis Repraesentans,* 1650. Courtesy of Geographicus Rare Antique Maps.

Copper Canyon Press is in residence at Fort Worden State Park in Port Townsend, Washington, under the auspices of Centrum. Centrum is a gathering place for artists and creative thinkers from around the world, students of all ages and backgrounds, and audiences seeking extraordinary cultural enrichment.

LIBRARY OF CONGRESS CATALOGING-IN-PUBLICATION DATA
Names: Levin, Dana, author.
Title: Now do you know where you are / Dana Levin.
Description: Port Townsend, Washington : Copper Canyon Press, [2022] |
    Summary: "A collection of poems by Dana Levin"—Provided by publisher.
Identifiers: LCCN 2021053276 (print) | LCCN 2021053277 (ebook) |
    ISBN 9781556596339 (paperback) | ISBN 9781619322509 (epub)
Subjects: LCGFT: Poetry.
Classification: LCC PS3562.E88953 N69 2022 (print) | LCC PS3562.E88953
    (ebook) | DDC 811/.54—dc23
LC record available at https://lccn.loc.gov/2021053276
LC ebook record available at https://lccn.loc.gov/2021053277

98765432 FIRST PRINTING

COPPER CANYON PRESS
Post Office Box 271
Port Townsend, Washington 98368
www.coppercanyonpress.org

ACKNOWLEDGMENTS

Gratitude to the editors of the publications where these poems first appeared, sometimes in different forms:

Academy of American Poets Poem-a-Day: "Instructions for Stopping"

Academy of American Poets Poets.org: "You Will Never Get Death / Out of Your System"

Air/Light: "January Garden"

The American Poetry Review: "How to Hold the Heavy Weight of Now," "Pledge," "2016: A Biography," "Your Empty Bowl"

The Best American Poetry 2021: "Immigrant Song"

Bullets into Bells: Poets & Citizens Respond to Gun Violence: "Instructions for Stopping"

Guesthouse: "The Birth and Death Corn," "Heroic Couplet"

Harvard Review: "For the Poets"

Houseguest, the *Guesthouse* blog: "Your Empty Bowl"

Kenyon Review: "Two Autumns, Saint Louis"

The Nation: "Immigrant Song"

New England Review: "Maybe"

The New Republic: "No"

Poetry Society of America: "You Will Never Get Death / Out of Your System"

Resistance, Rebellion, Life: 50 Poems Now: "You Will Never Get Death / Out of Your System"

The Sewanee Review: "Into the Next Eden"

The Slowdown: "You Will Never Get Death / Out of Your System"

Washington Square Review: "About Staircases"

The Yale Review: "Appointment"

Enormous thanks to Joseph Bednarik, Laura Buccieri, Elaina Ellis, Emily Grise, John Pierce, Jessica Roeder, Marisa Vito, Ryo Yamaguchi, and everyone at Copper Canyon Press, and to Michael Wiegers for the edits and encouragement and twenty-plus years of Yes.

To Mark Lombardi, Cherie Fister, and my colleagues in the humanities department at Maryville University: your warmth and welcome have been sustaining.

Erin Belieu, Gaby Calvocoressi, Victoria Chang, Matt Donovan, Janet Edwards, Carmen Giménez Smith, Louise Glück, Jay Hopler, Gary Jackson, Ted Mathys, Meghan O'Rourke, Bailey Schaumburg, Diane Seuss, Paul Tran, and G.C. Waldrep: comrades, readers, editors, suggesters, you offered buoys and direction.

To Brandon Brown and Melinda Freudenberger: thanks for being there for Murray the Cat.

To my sister, Caryn, for asking me to take the pledge, among a thousand other things—so grateful we walk this world together.

To John, for a second spring.

CONTENTS

NOW DO YOU KNOW WHERE YOU ARE

A WALK IN THE PARK

To be born again, you need
       an incarnation specialist—a team
from the Bureau of Needles
       to thread you through—
Your next life
       turns
on an axle of light—which Plato likens
       to a turning
spindle—what was that?
       I mean I *knew*

what a spindle was
       from fairy tales—how it could
draw blood
       from a testing finger, put a kingdom
to sleep—
       but what
did it actually do, how
       did a spindle look
in real life?
       I didn't know. As with
so many things:
       there was fact and there was

       a believed-in dream . . .

Everyone had them back
       in the ancient day,
spindles.
       When we had to weave
our living-shrouds
       by hand.

"A slender rounded rod
          with tapered ends," Google said. Plato's,
so heavy with thread,
          when viewed from the side,
looked like a top—
          though most diagrams assumed

          the hawk-lord view . . .
Moon thread, threads of the planets, earth thread.
          Your thread.
Everyone else's.
          Nested one
inside the other, a roulette
          machine—
If a thread could be spun from liquid light was what
          I kept thinking—
imagining a sluice
          of electric souls
between the earth-wheel's rims—
          there "I"

was a piece of water, Necessity
          wheeled it around—Necessity,
who was married to Time,
          according to the Greeks—
Mother of the Fates.
          Who would measure and cut your

          paradise/shithole extra life . . .

Well we all have ways of thinking about
          why,
metaphysically speaking,
          anyone's born—
though the answer's always Life's
          I AM THAT I AM

—how it hurls and breaks!
on Death's *No there*
        there . . .

—which sounded kind of Buddhist.
According to the teachings we were all
        each other's dream . . .

And soon able to vanish—
out of the real
        without having to die, whoever's
got the cash—to pay
        the brainier ones
to perfect
        a Heaven upload—to cut
the flesh-tether
        and merge

with the Cloud . . .

Well we all have ways of constructing
        Paradise.
To walk alone deep in thought
        in a city park
was mine
        for several minutes,
thinking about spindles.
        Before the vigilance
of my genderdoom

        kicked in—

And there it was, the fact
        of my body—
all the nerves in my scalp
        and the back of my neck,

alive—
        How it moved through space, how close
it had strayed
        toward concealing trees, my
female body—
        Jewish body—inside my
White body—dreaming
        it was bodiless

        and free . . .

        to decide:
how and when and if to fill the body's hungers—
        how and when and if to walk in thought
through the wilderness . . .

        before Death comes with its Fascist hat.

        Its Park Murder Misogyny hat.

        Its Year Ten in a Nursing Home stink
                hat—

        However spun
                my thread . . .

Anyway,
        it's peaceful here
in the park, at midday,
        if a little deserted. I've moved to the path that winds
closer to the street.
        Thinking again, as I always do,
about body and soul. How they
        infuse each other. How they
hate each other.
        How most people pledge allegiance

to one or the other.
How painful it was! To be
such a split

creature—

IMMIGRANT SONG

Bitter Mother

Blue, dead, rush of mothers,
conceal your island, little star.

Trains, hands, note on a thread,
Poland's dish of salt.

They said, The orphanlands
of America
       promise you a father—

The ship's sorrows, broken daughter,
the ocean's dark, dug out.

Silent Father

Rain, stars, sewage in the spill,
hush the river.

In your black boat, broken snake,
you hid. You sailed

for the meritlands of America,
dumped your name in the black
            water—

In the village they pushed the rabbi
to the wall—someone
            blessed the hunter.

Angry Daughter

One says No and the other
      says nothing at all—

Chicago, I will live in your museums
where Europe is a picture on the wall.

Obedient Child

I concealed my island,
my little star.

In my black boat I hid.
I hid in pictures on the wall.

I said, I am here in America,
your hero, your confusion,

your disappointment after all.
They said,

How did you end up so bad
in a country this good and tall.

INSTRUCTIONS FOR STOPPING

Say *Stop.*

Keep your lips pressed together
after you say the *p:*

(soon they'll try
to pry

your breath out—)

—

Whisper it
three times in a row:

Stop Stop Stop

In a hospital bed
like a curled-up fish, someone's

gulping at air—

How should you apply
your breath?

—

List all of the people
you would like
to stop.

Who offers love,
who terror—

Write *Stop*.
Put a period at the end.

Decide if it's a kiss
or a bullet.

TWO AUTUMNS, SAINT LOUIS

1. *Calvary Cemetery*

Driving up Union to get there, all the yard signs saying We Must Stop Killing Each Other—

A sign blaring CRISPY SNOOT—

An abandoned two-story with the windows blown out—a cooler and a bucket on the porch roof outside a second-story window—

At Calvary Cemetery, Groundskeeper Lambert, "like the airport": What are you looking for? Tennessee Williams. Say it again?

We asked to see the graves of Tennessee Williams, Dred Scott, and Kate Chopin; he obliged with the first two but as to the third, he hadn't heard of her.

On his own he showed us four things:

The hill where all the priests are buried—

The large hill empty of markers—

> "That's where the mass graves are, cholera, diphtheria, real Wrath of God stuff, we don't dig there—ever."

A giant wasp nest hanging in the crook of a cross-shaped headstone—

> "How close do you wanna get?"

The tomb where that old Saint Louisan with the two names is buried—

> How she had been in cotton and asked to be buried on the tallest hill overlooking the river, so she could watch the loading from on high—

Later, Janet says, "I can't find any record of that."

Lucas Hunt. There had been copper siding on the entry to her tomb, but thieves took it and sold it for scrap.

So too the giant Lincoln-penny medallion set in a nearby obelisk; some groundskeeper had even seen the man prying it out—stashed it in his backpack and took off running. You can see the empty circle and where the crowbar went in.

Janet says, "So someone steals a giant penny, but other people leave real ones on the headstone of Dred Scott."

The stones signify someone visited. Also flowers, beer, money, photographs, marijuana, toys, jewelry, clothes. People steal them, or they're picked up every two weeks and thrown away.

Animals that live at the cemetery: raccoons, coyotes, squirrels, hawks, foxes.

Paul, who comes every day and stays for hours, pulling flowers from the trash and redistributing them among the dead—

Fiery plastic flower adorning the stone of the playwright's sister, Rose—

Later, talking about Ferguson over mussels at Peacemaker's, nothing but White people in the room.

2. A Parade of Horribles

Dred Scott v. Sandford, 60 U.S. 393 (1856)

Pulling up to Cherie's and startling a deer grazing in the yard—
when it looked up, the shock
    of a long white arrow shot through its cheeks—

Shot clean through. As in the prank prop
Arrow Through the Head.
    And the deer—you could tell—had just

    healed around it and sought to walk peaceably
                    through the green corridors—

                    . . . and it is hardly consistent
                    with the respect due to these States,
                    to suppose that they regarded . . .

                    or, that when they met in convention to form
                    the Constitution, they looked upon them . . .
                    or designed to include them. . . .

                    It cannot be supposed that they intended
                    to secure to them rights,
                    and privileges,
                    and rank,
                    in the new political body. . . .

                    It cannot be believed . . .

                    For if they were so received, . . . it would
                    give to persons . . .
                    the right to enter every other State
                    whenever they pleased,

                    singly or in companies,
                    without pass or passport,
                    and without obstruction,

                    to sojourn there

                    as long as they pleased,
                    to go where they pleased
                    at every hour of the day or night—

and then it was gone, the wound and its arrow, vanishing back
                        into the suburban bracken—

3. Commerce

On Halloween, you don't get any candy until you tell a joke.

> Why did the clown go to the doctor?
>
> He was feeling funny.
>
> Why did the skeleton go to the barbecue?
>
> He was looking for spare ribs.
>
> Have you heard about the guy who got his whole left side
>   chopped off?

> > *John Wright, former assistant superintendent of the Ferguson-*
> > *Florissant school district, remembers a chain stretching across*
> > *a road to cut off access from the black city . . . to the . . . white.*
> > *"I tell people I'm from an apartheid town."*

4. Schnucks

"Well," she said, "you'd have to find out
        if it was just you or all customers,
        if it was only white customers or all customers,
        if it was only black baggers or all baggers,
        if it was just that Schnucks or all Schnuckses,
        if the manager at that specific store had made a rule
                after something happened,
        if it was an official policy or a culture of don'ts,

if the corporate offices had a rule about it
            as a matter of course,
you'd need to talk to each bagger, cashier, and manager
            at that specific Schnucks,
some white shoppers and some black shoppers,
even the young woman you say made a big show of it,
to know why baggers at Schnucks on Lindell
will bag
but won't hand you
your eggs."

5. Missouri Haibun

—gunning for deer rabbit turkey squirrel deals God gold fences you
treated your hunting dog better than your barn dog better than your wife
help workers daughters your Black daughters and Black sons your French
fur-trapping great-grand half-blood quarter-blood one-sixteenth denied
denied denied denied until a curious future daughter/son spits and ships
you off to ancestry.com—

            Was it a shock to you,
      the afterlife?
            Where no one
            was a king
                  in a White body—

6. Standing Outside the Fenced-In Parking Lot That Was Your Childhood Home

It's exciting to be living in the city that birthed
            T.S. Eliot
even though he was a casual
            anti-Semite

like so many of his class
        and breed—

L'shana tova, Tom!
        (my grandmother spits three times)
I stand here DLev,
        one of the roughs—aspirated, liberally
educated,
        shtetl-fed.

7. Election Day

At the post office mailing my book about Apocalypse to A. ("YES PLZ"),
while the postal clerk's got HOPE-FULL LIVING splayed facedown on
her desk—Privilege means getting to choose the hour of y(our) doom—

> "Does your package contain anything liquid, perishable, fragile, or
> potentially hazardous?"

> "There's poetry in there," I say. "Maybe that's hazardous—"

> "Poetry!" she says, brightening. "I like love poetry. I like woman-*scorned*
> poetry—" Then, leaning in: "I don't like that hatred poetry—" like
> she's telling a secret—

> HOPE-FULL LIVING. Could you find it on the web. Could you find
> it driving around Saint Louis (Confederate Drive, Plantation Drive,
> Creve Coeur, Heartbreak—   ,

8. Forest Park

Friends,
      ghosts, pneu-
matophores, "air
      roots,"
what Janet called
      "cypress knees," they
looked like knees, each
      a bent leg fused
shin to thigh, a cloak-
      huddled
hump in a crowd
      of clustered humps
approaching the bank, I
      "had not thought death
had undone so many" is what I
      thought as I
came upon them,
      all seeking succor, a lit arrival

      at Round Lake—

      which was really a pond
          and its fountain—

      which was really a lakelike
          heaven—

      someone's idea
          of municipal joy . . .

"To rub the heels
      with cypress resin
enabled one
      to walk on water," the Symbolicum said,

"since it makes the body light."

An American idea: that
        you could cross over—from heavy-chained

    to free—

    Who got what kinds of free. Who
            still believed . . .

Round Lake.
        Ringed by cypress,
a funerary tree.
        As in the maps
the Buddhists drew
        of Paradise—where you had to

    walk first
among the carrion birds,
        pick
through dog and corpse and the flesh
        between them,
in the graveyards
        of contested skin,
before you could reach
        the diamond center: a being

    of undifferentiated light—

Saturday, Saint Louis,
        seventy-four degrees.
At Forest Park,
        you can find restored riparian
habitats
        and steps

to a buried river behind a locked
            gate.
You can find bald eagles
            and butterfly weed
and the Angel of the Spirit of the Confederacy,
            a statue
dedicated
            fifty years after slaves were freed. An
ecology.
            I'm new here,
from the desert West.
            All the license plates say Show Me.

Saint Louis 2015–2016

2016: A BIOGRAPHY

I had wanted to think that America
was incidental, that I could go on with the same
lyric project, to lament the soul
in exile, having to endure the jail
of the body, what was
a president
to me.

YOU WILL NEVER GET DEATH / OUT OF YOUR SYSTEM

November 2016

How old is the earth? I asked my machine, and it said: Five great extinctions, one in process, four and a half billion years.

It has always been very busy on Earth: so much coming and going! The terror and the hope ribboning through that.

Death, like a stray dog you kick out of the yard who keeps coming back—its scent of freedom and ruin—

    Some people love death so much they want to give it to everyone.

    Some are more selective.

    Some people don't know they're alive.

                                    —

Metabolic system, financial system, political system, ecosystem—systems management, running around trying to put out fires—

Sodium nitrate. Sodium benzoate. Butylated hydroxyanisole (to keep the food from rotting). Plastic (surgery). Botox, Viagra, cryo-chamber—

Voting backward, into what
has already died—

Voting Zombie in the name of "change"—

And everywhere in fortune cookies, the oracular feint of a joke future—

where death is the trick candle on the victory cake.

—

Some truths are hard to accept. Especially when they won't budge beyond a couplet.

Especially when they won't tell you if they mean you well, if they herald freedom or ruin—

You! You and Death! Lovers who just can't quit. That's how we make the future—

as change goes viral.

HEROIC COUPLET

Out of range of North Korean missiles here in Saint Louis—I looked on a map. Out of range, but not of the secondary ash cloud, if the Yellowstone supervolcano explodes. Or the old nuclear-waste dump meets underground landfill-fire a couple of miles from the airport. Definitely in range of drought, storm, flood, famine, pandemic, riot, economic collapse, dirty bomb, mass shooting, rape, carjack, burglary, stroke, heart attack, cancer, mechanical failures of various kinds—

> *O Bomb in which all lovely things*
> *moral and physical anxiously participate*

Thinking about Corso and Ginsberg being chased out of a meeting of an antinuke group at Oxford by audience members throwing shoes, because Corso read, "O Bomb I love you / I want to kiss your clank eat your boom," "I want to put a lollipop / in thy furcal mouth"—his poem saying, Why fear Bomb? It's just another kind of Death, which will come for us all, generous friend—

> #WeAreToast

But I'd wanted to write about feeling lost, before I woke up thinking about the nation. How finally—when? A week ago! Eons ago! Ten executive orders ago!—at the end of my session with Jensen, I said I'd felt for months like someone had jammed a helmet and breastplate over me and I'd been trying ever since to get it off. He said, "What if you're not supposed to take it off? What if you're supposed to find a sword to go with it?"

> I felt the cogs of Era turn—
> and had to pop a Klonopin—

NO

Hoping to just live quietly unnoticed—holed up

smoking pot and listening to old music

after work, trying to wait out

the regime—dreaming of tyrants in exhausted

sleep, sick

     of having to think—

Trying the long view—in which years breathe

and the Great Wheel always turns, but

so much damage done as ash and seed

change places, as they always do—was that

still true? When you could

     see the fires of ending spreading, would you

get to live—in greater days when No

would blossom into Yes and Closed

pried—open-hearted -throated -minded, would you

get to live—as you thought you once

     did—

PLEDGE

a portion of days
Santa Fe, January–April 2017

JANUARY 29, 2017

Still in bed, eyeing out the window a crow flying around the big pine that is the crows' sentry, how they've stripped the needles from the very top branches—to see more clearly? To mark it "mine"?

A flash just now of sitting up in this bed in a whole new room come June, in Saint Louis.

In the living room here the roof still leaks even after two visits from the roofers. Put old cat litter buckets under leaks and went to sleep and woke up to a pace of thwoks—

Reminded me of N.'s final project for Hertel's Art and Environment class all those years ago at Pitzer: how he'd made a drum and set it up under a peppertree in the chaparral that bordered campus in those days, and the whole class trooped out there to see it.

N. said something about Time, about man-invented time and the time the earth gave us, how he wanted Time to naturally mark itself by the falling of leaves and other natural debris on the drum.

And I remember thinking a falling leaf wouldn't make very much sound on the skin of a drum—

THWOK—go the water drops from the roof into the kitty litter buckets, THWOK—time dropping its little stones of passage—

My project had been getting T. to build me a freestanding door in a frame, a door you could put anywhere, that could open and close. We set it up in the middle of the vast soccer field, and the class trooped up there to see it—

Spontaneously the students formed a line and one by one opened the door, each announcing an intended destination—"I'm going to Hawaii!"—and stepping through—

As if declaring it could make it so. *I'm going!* and a portal opened through space, powered by wish and imagination—while Time beat time on the skin of the world.

JANUARY 31

Woke up and entirely skipped my pledge, skipped it all day, skipped it until after evening drinks and nachos with old student S., who is caught between the call of job security and the call to write—who is not writing. I told her about my own current difficulties with writing and said, "You know, my sister made me take this pledge—" and I told her to take it too.

Pledge: to write every day for twelve weeks about your feelings (blech).

Murray the Cat rubbing the edge of this journal so vigorously, to mark it his—while I write about skipping and extolling the pledge—

Venus so big and bright in the cold western sky as we walked out of Del Charro's—every constellation bright in the cold dark sky as I walked to my front steps, even the Seven Sisters—

And then a mental flash: August's imperium, enormous cumulonimbus clouds processing from the southwest in fleets.

FEBRUARY 4

Coffee with some old students. Talking about Fame, Ambition's fickle, glitzy paramour—

Remembering then the body that had knelt and the head that had bowed under the lama's hand.

Telling them about the Tibetan Buddhist relics we'd toured, my sister and I, years ago. Bending to peer at a tiny scrap of parchment said to feature the original written word of a woman saint. I remember that most clearly: the tiny scrap of parchment big as the pad of my thumb and the script on it, curl of black flame.

It was all that was left!—of her handwriting—

At the end of the touring line, there sat the lama. And you were to kneel and receive his blessing. What had I prayed for as I knelt, I prayed to be a messenger—to record whatever wanted to stream through, regardless of it being met with failure, silence, or star—

Even though, like my students, I wanted to be an acknowledged prophet. I'd prayed for it to be okay to be a vessel.

FEBRUARY 5

I wake up midthought, as if all night I've been in an eighteenth-century coffeehouse, arguing about the State.

As if I've been hunkered in a D.C. apartment with federal workers planning insurrection—

As if all night, in sleep, I've been arguing with fellow travelers about conspiracy versus incompetence, about whether we can liken what's going on to Germany, 1933—

Then Murray climbs up and settles inside my left arm for his morning snuggle. I tell him he is a good cat, the best kitty ever, how sorry I am that he is sick, that he cannot come with me when I move, that I must hasten his end. Sometimes I wonder if I should just take him off all intervention now, so I can really *get* how sick he is—and feel less . . . guilt? Grief? About euthanizing him—

FEBRUARY 10

How am I feeling.

Bum tooth, sinus infection, the seemingly endless regimen of penicillin—and the whole shoulder/thoracic thing that's been bothering me since November. Vise around the chest.

On Facebook we are taking turns alarming and exasperating and bolstering each other, helping and hindering each other, advising and scolding each other, every once in a while inspiring each other, deflating each other, frightening each other, encouraging each other, sharing action items and telephone numbers and horrible news articles, and every once in a while someone still posts a picture of a baby or food.

February 16

Watching Murray uncommonly spry for the first time in a long while, tossing a rubber band under the kitchen table, playing his game of obstacle chair—

How can I possibly kill him when there is so much life in him?

Outside, the big sky—pinpoint diamonds in the clear black night—Orion, Pleiades, Big Dipper, Cassiopeia—

Cat Nation Sky Trump Stars

March 5

All last week in Northern California, walking on the haul road in Fort Bragg with C., stopping a moment to snap pics of vivid, tiny blue flowers dotting the sides of the road—

Posting one close-up to Instagram, saying, "That to which I pledge allegiance."

Thinking about *pledge,* the etymology, what was it? Anglo-Norman, meaning *hostage, guarantor.* Then *security, bail, guarantee.* "To be responsible for, to vouch for." Then "a solemn commitment to do or to refrain from doing something: a promise, a vow."

Thinking about this pledge journal—is everything I write about, then, that to which I pledge allegiance?

Writing, and a tiny blue flower, holding me hostage!

MARCH 6

Sitting with C., drinking early morning coffee, talking about not being up for the task of being us in this postelection environment, conflict avoidant and inward and hermetic, burrowers, hiders—having come through childhood already exhausted, by the blasts and craters of a sky-god father.

Drinking coffee strong and thick and loaded with half-n-half the way we like it—getting to the dregs, and in my cup seeing that the oracular grounds had painted a scene: a figure at the base of a mountain, two pines at the pinnacle behind her, bent over a desk, or a sacrificial altar.

MARCH 8

Yesterday I imagined setting up a Twitter account called LOVE, whose bio is LOVE, and all I do is tweet love at Donald J. Trump.

Examples:

You are enough.

Inclusivity = more applause, Donald J. Trump!

Benevolent rulers are loved even beyond the
    grave— #love

That the Republic holds. That the bombs stay in their bays in the earth's deep pockets. That the bigots slink back into their diselected holes.

MARCH 9

Visited M.'s class today. A student asked me about the shapes
of my stanzas, their heavy indents, their short and long lines,
and as I was talking, I realized: New Mexico! The vast page of
its sky! For nineteen years, the open field—

in which thought and image have bloomed and chimneyed and
changed and faded and bloomed . . .

Venturing out on very cold nights to go in the garage and put
laundry in the dryer—giant Orion sharp and bright as if its stars
were made of crystal ice—and before night, to the west, Venus
and moon-sliver above extending lines: vermilion, purple, pink,
green, gray, gold.

MARCH 18

Sitting on the front porch with Murray, his last week on this
earth, his breath is starting to stink and his back legs aren't at
all steady—the other day catching sight of him standing in the
hallway and so startled: as if his face was sagging right off his
skull.

MARCH 20

I haven't been sleeping well, but then last night I let myself
object strenuously to this move, to leaving New Mexico, to
killing my cat, to leaving my friends. *I don't want to, I don't
want to,* hot hot tears—and then I slept.

MARCH 23

Days of placid warmth and tree buds and blue blue sky every day a paradise of porch napping for Murray the Cat, today the martial spring winds gusted in, now all stormy and even rain and the temp's dropped twenty degrees in the last two hours.

Once I lived in a different part of town, and Murray would walk the low adobe walls separating each studio apartment from its neighbor, sometimes even then a foot would slip—he was always kind of clumsy for a cat, though now I wonder if that was congenital, he was always an oddly shaped creature, with his barrel chest and harelip and fucked up jaw so he looked like a vampire, his two fangs hanging like icicles outside his mouth.

Which is to say today he is alive and tomorrow he will not be, the week's been warm and languid and now it's cold and blustery, how after months of eyeing the Saint Louis poem notes with a mix of suspicion and helplessness and doubt I have suddenly whipped through a draft, when the sun was warm and Murray was dying—

All gates open to whatever energy is trying to flow through them—the way blood's arrival and departure sluices through the heart.

MARCH 25

BKF posting to my Facebook page, "There has been no greater cat in poetry since Christopher Smart's Jeoffry." Glorious epitaph!

Before the vet came yesterday to help him die, I took the collar off Murray's neck and said, "You're free!" Upon which he climbed into my lap and fell asleep.

APRIL 12

What makes a sound on the skin of a drum? The collection of little stones and sea glass and shells on the shelf—

The way at some point I place them into a circle (emptiness in the middle)—

But today I made a compass, with the heart-shaped quartz at the center and polished stones and sea glass raying off in four directions—

"Everything's all dissolving," I wrote to G.C.: cat, home, norms, nation?

Thinking about a walk I took with P. thirty years ago, down to the Piscataqua River—early spring, coats but no hats, talking earnestly about love and pain and being human beings with feelings—

"Thank you for being a human with feelings with me," I wrote today on P.'s Facebook page, her body dissolving—dying of cancer.

Sitting now on the front porch with only a ghost of a Murray, leaning against the wall warming in the sun, thinking, "I don't want to feel that, I'm too tired and overwhelmed to feel that—" closing my eyes.

APRIL 15

Cleaning out campus commences—all efforts to sell the college, save the college, failed. Writing to Ch.: "I want to get that wall hanging you made me—hope it's still outside my old office—" where I'd hung it up years ago, and left it behind when I quit to start teaching half the year in Saint Louis. A little act of defiance, if the school overlords ever walked the halls of Benildus: how they'd encounter three vertical columns of FUCK cheerily printed eighteen times amid blooms and leaves on cloth.

APRIL 17

Dozing. Hypnagogic flash: I'm instructing a young woman on the installation of enormous poems stenciled on a gallery wall. I tell her that when she's finished each poem, she has to take up a handful of wet earth and punctuate the poem with two mud seals, perfectly round, at the upper left and right corners of the poem-field. "This way," I say, "you are announcing: 'I am here, and I am made of earth.'"

APRIL 22

Opening the sliding glass door and screen to the back deck, everything looks so abandoned and lonely, no container garden this year, no cat on a mat among the Santa Fe flowers—

How I left all the doors open until winter wouldn't let me, letting in pollen and seeds and dead leaves and dust and crawling bugs and flying bugs and even sometimes a bird, a mouse, some other cat, so Murray could come and go at will—

Texting with old student B. about this pledge journal—my twelve weeks done! Would I shape it, would I share it? Its nakedness thrills and troubles me—

What does it mean to be a messenger? What is dignity?

"Maybe what we need right now is not to be held at arm's length," B. said. "Maybe what we need is to feel a poet's love for her dead cat. Haha! But seriously."

"Love and grief never get old, Dana Levin! They change and reappear too much for that!"

Cat Nation Sky Trump Clouds

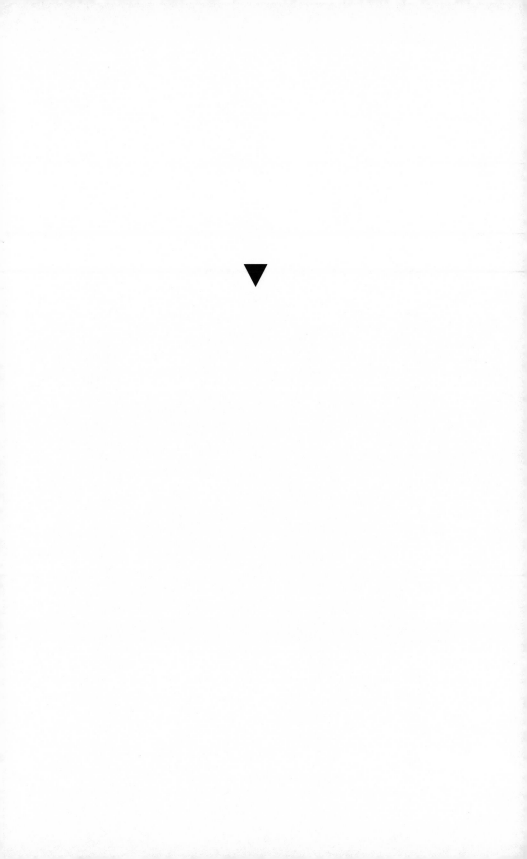

HOW TO HOLD THE HEAVY
WEIGHT OF NOW

She said, "You just made this gesture with your body—"
and opened her arms as if she could barely fit them
around an enormous ball—

"Make that shape again," she said, and so I did. "Now
let it change," she said, and I did—

slowly closing the space between my arms, fingertips
converging until they touched—

I watched my hands turn together, align pinkie-side to
pinkie-side, I watched

my palms open, pushing gently forward, leading my
body forward, I watched them

let a bird go, I watched my hands
        make

        an offering—

FOR THE POETS

To post, to share, to tag, to tweet, to have an audience for feats, Beowulf *granted the glory of winning,* Grendel *driven under the fen-banks, fatally hurt,* and the whole panoply of insulted Greeks, Agamemnon *the most grasping man alive,* but *Who if I cried out would hear me amongst the angelic orders* is the common condition, if only three people like a tweet does anything you offer sound in the forest? The history of civilization is replete with selfies, from pharaonic monoliths to portraits hanging in the Louvre, LUCIUS WAS HERE scratched in Latin on Colosseum walls, even the earliest handprints in the famous caves, we've always been Tommy's *SEE ME, FEEL ME, TOUCH ME, HEAL ME* climbing platforms to sashay the wealth, not plunder now but diamond contacts, accolades and golden "news," the flashy bling of being seen, such

dread and hope and fear to hope that the work will live in some greater way in other minds, the confrontation with Time and wanting to matter while inside it, *I'm Nobody! Who are you?* Miz D's morning cleanse or Uncle Walt's Jupiter tonic *I celebrate myself,* which is to say I was heading into one last student reading at a college I was leaving, to hear first poems about earth and sex and blood and stars, about the great forces and the dispossessed, parents, harm, and the Boot of the State, why, I thought, do any of us do any of this, because (and then verse came, such as it was):

> I was here, I
> lived in it, I
> died in it, this shit
>
> Paradiso—

MAYBE

was about all that I could muster—on the question
of whether this world, which I prefer to think of in the past

tense, will flourish—though the first of the last fires hasn't even
started yet—has it?

Maybe the past tense because it implies
survival—*back then* plus *but now,* as if the future

had already happened and you—you!—had made it out
alive—

into midday living room peace—
into two o'clock April light, you and a trailing

coleus—survivor too!—each leaf like a dab
of dried blood
on a scalloped pad

of green . . .

Sirens, in the distance, fading. Sirens
in the distance, above a wreck of ships, perched

where literature starts
with war, and lost men, heroes

enticed to death by birds
with the heads of girls, myth opening its blood-
drenched

wings—

Maybe it wasn't Future Death hounding me but
　　　　Past Ends—not popular Apocalypse but

cracked Atlantis, golem
　　　　Ozymandias, all the millions millions really dead

in ruined capitals gone to ash and dream—Maybe it was my
　　　　mother's mother's
　　　　　　　scapegoat trauma blood

　　　　keening—

And suddenly—I could see them!—every empire that ever
　　　　rose and fell spread out on discs

across an infinite plane called Absolute Now like
　　　　records spinning—all playing the same song,

track by track—Ruin
　　　　by Better Tech, Ruin by Hubris, Ruin

by Appetite Amok—and from this vantage History
　　　　looks like a choice, and I have to ask, now, in the present
　　　　tense, Why

　　　　choose the past

　　　　as the future—

THE BIRTH AND DEATH CORN

a ballad

Yesterday I went to see Jensen, and while I was on the table, he told me the story of the Birth and Death Corn. While he held the back of my head, probing my fucked up neck with his fingers. While I was coming off S.'s grief because J. left her, D.'s grief because R. left him, because D.'s father died and grief spun out reactive until he stood in tears at the bottom of my stairs. I'd had a laundry basket in one arm and D. in the other, he was about to vanish into a cell in Christ in the Desert, my Jewish Buddhist friend. And I was feeling so scared of walking into the future—when the present felt so dark and changed—

A couple he'd worked with. The mother in labor and the baby's heart stopping. The father so freaked out he called Jensen from the room where they were jumping the baby, trying to get it to start—*race race jump* and its battery going, "But the doctors aren't happy—" the father said to Jensen on the phone. Because the brain was long gone. By law, they'd have to keep it hooked up for four days, until damage could be itemized, asserted as fact—but everyone knew the soul-baby was gone, and they were tending a meat balloon.

The four days passed and they let the body go. And then—as he prodded my neck and moved my skull around like a cap shoved wrong on top of a bottle—they sowed her umbilical into the ground. Mixed with seed corn and the mother's placenta. And nine months later, when the new corn was ready, they mashed it with water, making a pulp—Jensen was there, he told me about it. While I lay there so scared of walking into the future, how the family gave everyone who'd gathered a cup—and, he said, everyone drank her. They drank her, and to me it was the opposite of grief's black milk—they told stories about the soul-baby's lineage. How her spirit rode the stories like a current, how the drinking and the telling were the same. To be remembered, he said, and to nourish. And then he moved one hand from my neck to my sacrum, and with the other pushed a finger deep into my belly, into the crossroad hole in my network of scars—once I'd been a baby who'd been born dying. And really, isn't that how each of us is born? Grow now, and die in the future. He told me about the Birth and Death Corn.

ABOUT STAIRCASES

I

To be human is to reflect upon your position in space: on a
roof it's called Seeking, in a basement Paranoia—especially
with a telescope. On the leather couch, behind the blue
door, in a row of doors down a long, white hallway, windows
chicken-wired glass: thirty years ago I told Dr. C., *I feel like
I'm being haunted by my four-year-old self, I feel like I'm being
haunted—inside my body.* Jury-rigged staircases, one atop the
other, in my psych-room construct inside-body: on the roof
it's called Save Me, in the basement Don't Kill Me—up and
down, the ghost-child raged. Thinking then,

> Inconsolable Escher—you never wanted to climb
> the fucking stairs, ever.

2

To be human is to try to change your position in space:
hide-and-seek, king-of-the-mountain, all the drugs I did to
stay awake inside dreams—Elevators, the philosopher wrote,
do away with the heroism of climbing; no longer is there
virtue in living up near the sky. In mythology class, we dis-
cuss ambition: the falling boy, his melted wings—late night
dorm room pot-cloud question: how many human means of
ascension? D. lost interest,

> took up his guitar—
> money, beauty, talent, force.

3

Can change be achieved by contesting your position in space?
The brave ones try it: climbing into trees marked for clear-
cut, refusing to move to the back of the bus. What we expe-
rience as conflict, the mythographer wrote, the Great Mother
perceives as parts rearranging—but is harmony possible in
a kingdom of ladders, where there's always a foot coming
down on a neck? A poet asks: What would be a horizontal

      notion of progress? (wider and wider

         rings of kindness—)

4

In a movie, a man repents murder by climbing to the top of
Amazonian falls, lugging in a net his suit of armor. And when
one of the priests, after hours of watching him slog through
mud, lifts a machete and hacks the ropes—well it feels so true:
how our liberated man tries to dive for the armor. But I'm
thinking now about letting it go. About Georges Guétary
in *An American in Paris,* singing "I'll Build a Stairway to
Paradise." In top hat and tails. On stairs that light up when
pressed by a toe. He climbs between dancers descending in
rivers, dancers who swan, diaphanous, down—once, a war
was over and the stairs were lit: such

      going up and down

        with flourish—

JANUARY GARDEN

| Woke up with: | *the minute I let "I love you" touch me, trees* |
| | *sprouted from my hair—* |

| Woke up with: | *Zeus fatigue—*   (what ails the nation) |

| Woke up with: | *the soul a balm, a lozenge, yet another* |
| | *pill-shaped thing—* |

| Woke up and | recalled nothing—   took a walk in winter air— |

in the January garden. No one
on benches—

And then remembered—with a bolt—how I'd been
titling a poem in my sleep:

>   *A Little Less, Day after Day, Bomb after Bomb*

And just as I remembered, I passed a young woman
at a picnic table, writing in a journal—

And she held—so help me!—a pen shaped
like a bone—

And I heard the poem:

>   *Each of us, by nature, a killer—*

>   *Each of us, by nature,*
>   *picking something to practice*

>   *mercy on—*

YOUR EMPTY BOWL

I

The doctor makes a curving incision in the left top
      back of my skull and

lifts the cap—"What area
      am I here to work on?" But I

      just want to wish his son a happy birthday—

It had been my aim, the reason I'd
      walked right in

      to this Doctor dream—In the morning,

        —

my neighbor reports from his year
      of losses: a well dried up and the threat of fire, the offer

of haven, now his sister's
      stroke— "I feel," he said, "like a bowl

      that God keeps scooping out—"

It made me nervous, how emptied he was—how every few months
      a place, a face, that mattered to him,

      crumbled into gone—

My solution was ridiculous, so I extolled it with fervor. I said,
      "You should meditate

on an empty bowl, you should *go outside* and sit
        with an empty bowl *in real*

life—" For weeks,

I'd been battering him over the head with hope and will—as if
        hope and will

                                —

        could make magic—

And the little man with the bowl in Central Park that spring thirty years ago
        when I did not know

        how to change my life—

What a strange little man he was, so small and the bowl
        so enormous—

He could barely get each arm around it, as he
        picked me out of the throng

on the new spring Lawn, I must have looked
        drifty and aimless—

"Make a wish," he said, standing under me, "Ring the bell—Don't listen
        to the neighbors—"

I looked down
        into the giant mixing bowl, and in the bowl a bell—

And *what did I want, what did I want,* I'd just, the night before
        on Second Avenue,

        walked by a man

—

stabbed in the chest

Shine-blur of streetlights in the blood soaking his shirt—

People three deep in a wide ring around his breaths—

A three-foot distance between his bleeding body and everyone
      watching him bleed, and no one

            extending a hand, no one speaking—no one

            breaking through the circle to say, "What? What?" then

sirens, and I knew
            someone had called. And I stood there,

      outside a ring of forty living motionless people watching one
            dying in the middle, and all of us there

            really needing some help—

            I wanted, I thought, to leave

—

      New York—

"That's it!" the little man cried, as I picked up the bell
      and rang it and rang it—

While another man, tall and lanky (the two of them
      must've been a team), into my ear

with a hiss and a lean, "Your wish
        will never come true," and the little man shouting, "DON'T

LISTEN
        TO THE NEIGHBORS—"

And the tall man striding away. And the little man
        then offering me

        a gamble:

                "You give me a dollar, you get back ten,
                You give me a ten, you get back a hundred,
                whatever you give me, you get back
                        ten times ten—"

So I gave him a ten. And a week later made a surprise
        hundred bucks showing slides
for an auction
        at Sotheby's—

2

What story am I trying to tell.

The one
        of unexpected loss and the one

        of unexpected gain, I guess.

The story of No, and then the story

                        —

        of Yes—

At Sotheby's, I don't remember
        what was for sale. I remember

the wound of money and the fact of it—chasing it, getting it, losing it,
        needing it—like blood or breath.

I thought
        if my neighbor sat with an empty bowl, maybe

he'd get an idea—some kind of American *Aha!*—
        to fix everything—

But he could sit
        for an entire night, glean nothing

        but a bowl of dew—not even

                        —

        a poet could eat it.

Before the ambulance arrived, a woman
        broke through the ring and ran to the wounded

body. She knelt
        in the blood in the street and took up

the stabbed man's hand—which is when I
        walked away. Just like me, to stay

for the bleeding but not the healing.
        To tell a friend

to sit outside with an empty bowl
        when he confides his loss—why didn't he

sock me in the mouth—why didn't I
    take up

                —

    his hand—

Should've rung the bell and wished for something else—

Should've taken
    my own advice and gone outside to sit

with an empty bowl in *real*
    life—

    wait for whatever my *Aha* . . .

Happy birthday! I'd wanted to wish
    the boy in my dream, Happy birthday! Happy birthday! Before I was

waylaid
    by the Father of Surgery, who set my skull-top

    down like a cap, and advanced

with his silver needles
    on the gray lobes of my open brain, saying, "I'm just

    going to make

                —

    an adjustment—"

APPOINTMENT

1

Jensen cracked my recalcitrant neck and I felt, finally, that I
was fully facing the can't-see of the future—

He said he felt that a whole new person was trying to be born
from inside me—the way an island wells up from the ancient
crust, all lava and steam, all heat and fire and mineral. That's
how I saw it, as he said it.

He said, Can you let yourself be completely rewired—

He said, This is what the earth is doing, we have to get
ready—

He said, Something primordial eons ago ended up in you, so
it could say something.

2

I found him because Walter, my osteopath, was leaving for
medical school. Walter, who one day maneuvered my feet
and my legs and my hips so that I felt—extraordinary!—
what it was like to have normal posture and gait. I'd found
Walter through M., a Canadian expat I was doing Pilates
with. How had I found M.?

Santa Fe was like that: you'd make the rounds of healers, led
by word of mouth. Back then, Jensen had no listed phone
number or website or Facebook page. How had Walter
found him?

"Who does what you do?" I'd asked Walter when he told
me he was leaving. "Well . . ." he said slowly, "when I want

bodywork, I call Jensen." "Is he an osteopath?" I asked. "Well . . ." Walter said.

He gave me a phone number on a slip of paper. "He's trained as a chiropractor . . . but he does a lot of things."

3

Jensen was tall and lanky, and his face, in profile, looked like a hawk's. Carved hawk face on a very tall stalk: his human flower.

Telling him about feeling confused and troubled by my inclination to mine the personal past, when the collective present needs so much attention and aid—

He said, What if you could go back to before you were born—

He said, What if you could contact the barely Cro-Magnon ancestor—

And I saw her: young girl standing up on a branch near the top of a tree, facing a rising sun—she loved two things: dawn (it thrilled her!) and a piece of char, with which she could make a mark.

4

For most of the time I worked with him, his office was at his house. I say "office," but it was really a shaman's den. Feathers and drying plants hanging in various corners. Shelves and shelves of tinctures and herbs. Drums. Bones. Rocks. Flowers blooming or dying in a vase. Driftwood. Crystals. Postcards and framed pictures and tiles and figurines—gifts given over the years, you could tell, from people he had helped. Often they featured likenesses of one of the household gods: Buddha, Kuan-yin, Virgen de Guadalupe, Lord Ganesh. Or the teachers: Dalai Lama, Amma, John Lennon, Thích Nhất Hạnh, a tree, Martin Luther King Jr., Pope Francis, Calaveras. Totemic animals. The spirit figures you'd find in any American neo-pagan household, of which there were so many in Santa Fe, including mine.

5

I don't use the word "shaman" lightly.

Most of his patients were pregnant women or the dying—he specialized in people who were coming or going.

He told me he wanted a business card that said, "M. Jensen, Incarnation Specialist." And that's what he was for me.

6

How can I write about Jensen without writing about why I was there?

Every day, the map of scars incising my belly vanished from mind—every day, my fingers tracing its topography—

As they're doing now.

7

I leave the couch and the yellow legal pad where I was writing about why I worked with Jensen to come into the bedroom and open this journal to write about crying about writing about it.

Like a dog seeking a more secret hole in which to bury the bone—

Bone that I am trying to dig up—

And hadn't I dug it up once before, long ago, when I was young? A host of poems, dug out of the floor of the surgical theatre! Then buried in a book.

It sounds like a punishment, or a game: burying the bone so you have to dig up the bone, over and over—some kind of life assignment only your soul, or your dog, understands.

8

Today I realize that I have never looked up the actual biological thing that happened to me. So I Google it. The results are overwhelming.

I read about the history of blood transfusions, the history of neonatal surgery, the history of amniocentesis. I read obituaries of the doctors I should thank every day for my miraculous life.

I learn my condition was officially called Rh disease, or rhesus isoimmunization, "rhesus" for a similar factor found in rhesus monkey blood. I learn that "Rhesus (Rh) factor is an inherited protein found on the surface of red blood cells." In 1937 "the serum that led to [its] discovery was produced by immunizing rabbits with red blood cells from a rhesus macaque," and though Wikipedia doesn't report what happened to the rabbits, or the monkey, I imagine cages and syringes and masked humans long inured to animal fear and pain in the name of science.

I watch an animated film where the mother is covered in minus signs and the baby in plus signs. The mother's Y-shaped antibodies drop like wartime paratroopers into the portal where mother blood and baby blood meet. Suddenly the film zooms in on a mother macrophage—astounding, macrophages, the disease eaters in all of us!—looking like a battle jellyfish, enveloping and destroying an infant red blood cell inside its bell-shaped body and whisking the debris away.

I learn that I developed "hemolytic disease of the fetus and newborn," that it came about because my blood, like my father's, was positive for Rh factor, while my mother's was Rh negative. After two pregnancies with my Rh-positive sisters, my mother's Rh-negative body had developed enough immune sensitization to read me, her third viable fetus, as a disease to be eradicated, and this confirms everything about our difficult life together, my mother and me, always embattled, always a struggle *to get to live,* as myself—but that's a topic for another day.

I read about the development in the 1940s of exchange transfusion, the complete blood transfusion of the affected infant: the only known cure, which I myself endured.

I learn that Rh disease used to kill 10,000 infants a year in the United States alone. Then Dr. William Pollack developed a vaccine, a gamma globulin solution later known as RhoGAM. The vaccine was first tested, according to his *New York Times* obituary, "on volunteers at the Sing Sing Correctional Facility in Ossining, NY, and later on 600 Rh-negative women in clinical trials." It worked 99 percent of the time, was approved by the Food and Drug Administration and went on the market in 1969, four years after I was born.

9

Wasn't this too an exchange transfusion? The suffering of rabbits and monkeys and imprisoned "volunteers" and 600 women who faced or had experienced miscarriage and stillbirth, as my mother had, so that I and babies like me might stop suffering in utero and live? Was that what incarnation was: a suffering exchange—

10

Dream: I'm packing a suitcase. A male figure stands to my right, talking emphatically and pointedly, but I'm not really listening: I'm trying to stuff my large square maroon couch pillow into the suitcase. In life, it's way too big for a suitcase, if I want to pack anything else—

I manage to pack the pillow and feel some accomplishment as I successfully shut the top. Then I'm walking down a sidewalk in a city at night, alone, rolling the suitcase behind me. I'm a little concerned with how heavy it is, in terms of my own stamina, but brighten when I remember soon I can put it in checked luggage.

No one is about, in the night city. I roll along the perimeter of a park. And all at the edge where park meets sidewalk, fledglings have gathered, spreading their wings, too young really to make much display but displaying anyway—fledgling ravens and buzzards.

11

When I wake up, I think how those birds were the charnel-ground birds: carrion eaters, the earth purifiers—how the perimeter of the park was like one of the perimeters of a Tibetan Buddhist mandala, where you have to walk through the cemeteries on your journey to the center of light. But in the dream, I am walking by, on the way to somewhere else. Now I think I should've stopped and done the heroic thing: entered the park-mandala to weave through the cremation fires and feel my way through the long night of ghosts and dogs and bones—

But I didn't. Where was I going? (scars)

12

In the second month of my mother's last trimester, it became apparent that if they did not induce labor, the fetus inside her would die. Thus, six weeks early, yellow with jaundice, I was pushed into the light. And after the exchange transfusion, after the complete exsanguination of my old, diseased blood, and the stream of new blood—I started, once again, to die.

Neonatal necrotizing enterocolitis, a complication induced by the exchange transfusion: gangrene of the intestine, which, my mother later told me, was discovered by a surgeon based on the guess of Dr. Harold Brown, the beloved family pediatrician. Dr. Brown even rushed me into surgery before getting permission from my parents.

I was six days old. I weighed less than a bag of flour. The surgeon opened me up from sternum to pelvis and found the gangrenous ileum. He removed it and a portion of my intestine and attached a colostomy bag to my body. I spent the first two months of my life in an incubator, and I'm still attracted to the smallest, most bordered and ignored spaces of any room I am in—the one between the wall and a bed in a hotel room, for instance, or the empty space you might find under a landing and a stair—wanting to nestle in, right there.

13

In the neonatal ward, nurses put a feeding tube in each ankle—is that scientifically accurate, feeding through the ankle? It's what my mother told me; I wish she were alive to confirm.

When I sit on a yoga mat with my legs straight out in front of me and stretch forward to grab my ankles, I can feel the scars there, the depressions the feeding tubes left. My nails and my teeth are soft and discolored and easily chipped, because of how many antibiotics they gave me those first months of my life. My feet are pronated, and my legs below the knee look to me like they're misaligned with my thighs.

My mother once said that Dr. Brown, after the surgery, told my parents my legs might be affected and recommended leg braces to correct them, but my parents refused, remembering the shame and difficulty of President Roosevelt. Another time she told my oldest sister that they didn't get the leg braces because she didn't want me to look like the braced baby in the ads for March of Dimes.

And then, as I neared fifty, when knee and back and hip pain and numbness increased and began to alarm me, I wondered if my musculoskeletal issues stemmed from what had happened to me. Which is how I ended up with Walter, who, for a time, aligned my legs, and then forwarded me to M. Jensen, Incarnation Specialist.

14

I let him cradle my head in his two hands for what seemed a universe of minutes.

Sometimes this cradling would stop flat everything clattering around in my skull and I would feel like pure awareness, curious, alert, awake—

I always think of this as my essential soul state, before neurosis wells, before the needs and discomforts of the flesh reassert themselves: pure awareness, interested and bemused—by what it means to be alive and aware, in a body—

Incubators in 1965 were like human terrariums. In the photo I have, taken by my father, I'm lying on my stomach asleep and massively diapered, or bandaged, or both. I face a closed round porthole bigger than my little head, and there's a closed round porthole at my bandaged feet: here's where the gloved hands reached in to touch me—

15

Jensen's large open expressive hands.

16

Sometimes he would tap his cupping fingers around the base of my skull and reposition my head with sudden precise assertive movements, muttering all the while.

He muttered in tongues, when he worked on me. It was no language I could recognize. I never asked about it.

When he resorted to the tactics of chiropractic and something in my skeletal system released, he'd snap his fingers in answer. *Pop—snap!* Call and response.

Sometimes he cradled my sacrum for what seemed a universe of minutes. All my conscious focus would assemble there, and I would calm.

Sometimes he would push a finger deep into the pit of my deepest scar.

He held me. Maybe just this was the healing, outside the portholes and gloved hands and glass house into which I had once been deposited, after a knife wounded me so I could live.

17

Sometimes we would talk while he worked on my scarred and misaligned body. Mostly we talked about the end of the world.

With absolute certainty in its imminence, we talked about it. We were in complete accord. It felt comforting to share our certainties about extinction, this healer and this healed, us.

We believed in the power and resiliency of the earth. We weren't sure people would make it into the next age.

One time he told me his son worked in national security, and I didn't believe him. Then he showed me a photo. It was like looking at Jensen in an alternate universe: same hawk face, younger, in military dress. Something like bars, or medals, pinned to his breast.

18

One time he said, Guess what the number one concern in national security circles is— Terrorism? No. Nukes? No. "What?" I asked. Pandemic.

He stopped working on me and stood and looked into my face, my eyes. We have no idea what is going on, he said.

Then he leaned his hawk face forward and I closed my eyes again.

He said viruses are the way Mother Earth finds out what is happening in her children, that viruses are readers. Based on the information viruses gather, he said, the earth injects change into the ecosystem.

He tells me that viruses are responsible for the development of higher consciousness. Sit up—he says, and I do, and he places some kind of board behind my back. Did you know that between forty and eighty percent of our genetic code comes from ancient viruses? Lean forward—he says, and I do. "Where'd you read that?" I ask, and fully expect him to cite some other suspect hippie healer. In a journal called *Cell*, he says. Later I look it up and it's completely scientifically legit.

He replaces the board behind my back with his hand, his fingers pushing into my spine, midback. Cross your arms over your chest—he says, and I do. Suddenly he drops me back and—*pop!* His fingers snap.

He starts to position my head in order to crack my neck. I brace and then immediately go into panic-quell mode, trying to relax my body, praying he won't paralyze me. This happens at every visit, any time he readies to adjust my neck.

He never paralyzes me. The world never ends.

19

I keep thinking about the dream.

Next to "maroon pillow" I write: marooned.

I wonder if I am dreaming about my own heavy body, a suitcase I'm lugging around while marooned inside it, body that is both me and not me—ever aware of the split between the bag of meat and the animating spirit, having to be the *I* they make together, what was that *I,* that psychoid thing—

I's fate was to be a bridge and the awareness crossing it; its cross was to believe it was a fortified castle, a king.

Brightening up at the prospect of putting it in checked luggage!

Or am I dreaming about poetry, marooned inside me—I'd been having so much trouble writing, accepting what I was writing, being afraid to write because someone would see it (after four books!), with publishing like an invitation to attack or to silence that I couldn't possibly withstand, some kind of midlife paralysis going on for months and months and months and months—

It was like redoing my time in the womb, except this time I was the mother, trying to kill what I was in the midst of making.

Next to "maroon pillow" I write: the "useless" thing I value is marooned inside my body as I lug it past the carrion birds—

Fledgling death birds, eaters just beginning. Stamping and parading along the edge of the park-mandala, daring me to enter, spreading out their finalizing wings—

The way we imagine death is the way we experience birth: a harrow through the dark, and then a light—

All the little deaths you have to walk through, in order to be born and born and born.

20

Jensen pushed down hard on my clavicles on either side of my neck as I wept—

He said, Can you let yourself be completely rewired—

He said, This is what the earth is doing, we have to get ready—

Each of us alone inside our bodies, each of us marooned, in the suffering exchange, while the world burns—

I'd been feeling so paralyzed by Lord Time, how he numbered forward unswayed by human hope or need or aspiration, riding his stolid horse Death-My-Fate—

Later on the phone I tell my sister about it. "Maybe," she says, "the message of your life is that you can come through trauma and be okay"—an idea that completely floors me.

21

In my journal I write:

> *You're afraid because you're already*
> *dead, really, when you think about it.*
> *And since you're already dead, don't you just*

> *want to live—*

The heroic narrative. Did you know that in ancient Greek, the word *hero* and the name *Hera* are closely related: Hera, mother goddess, who watched over women bearing children—

As if to be a hero is to simply be a child of a mother—

The cervix opening its round door—

A sound welling up through the throat.

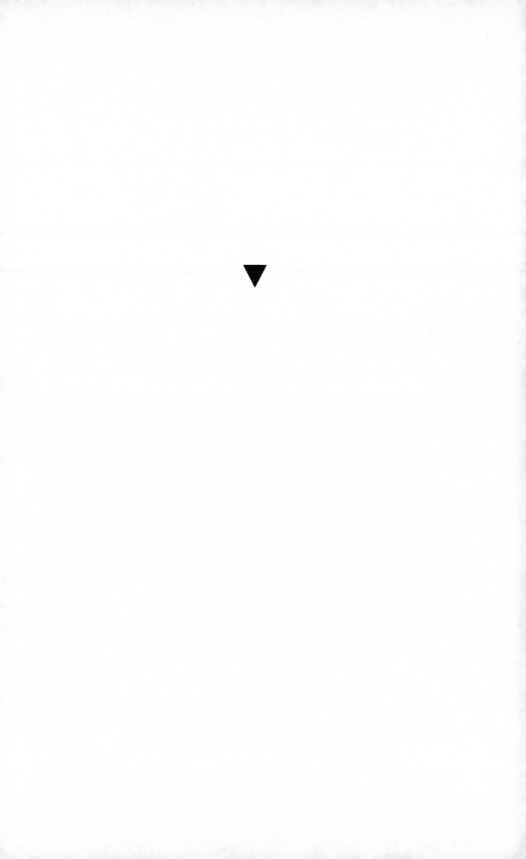

INTO THE NEXT EDEN

I was supposed to go back to the sea
    but plague prevented me.

In a city by a river no ship could take me
    and planes, well—

I stayed home for days with weekend drives
    to see my love,

    who didn't live with me.

Night cranks up its float of stars. They inch
    and tarry.

—

I was supposed to go back to the sea but nature
    prevented me.

It said, "Sit right down and let me
    clear the air—"

The sudden blue
    of the natural sky after years

    behind the smoke of money.

Mother Nature, who had had it
    with us—

    that was my theory.

So economical, how she laid us and all our wrecking
    low.

—

In another world I'd perched
        on petrified lava, watching the sea go.

I wanted to snatch each bit I saw and secure it
        in a book of glass—

        A rock in tide. Someone
                on the opposite cliff, smoking.

        A schooner cloud.
                Its reflection appearing—

        in a book transparent and indestructible.

        Would the book even make it
                into the next Eden.

—

I watched as a plant watches, rooted
        and waving in wind—

One of those scrubby plants you can't believe
        blooms from a cliff—

Sturdy miracle. Flexible and porous
        so change can get in . . .

The sea never stopped happening, it unfurled
        over and over

its massive rose—

love and death

love and death

love and death

beating the cliff down
to a nub.

—

I was supposed to go back to the sea
and so I've come.

Standing again inside my mind
on Big River Beach—

There, river tide and ocean tide
push and marry—

Seals swim up the river's finger
for as long as there's salt—

Standing again as I stood that day,
watching a mother—a baby

against her breasts, facing out—

eyes round, mouth round
as an o—

"It's the first time she's seeing the sea!"
the mother said, when she saw me watching—

The ocean wind blew our long hair
straight back—

We stood as flags pitched in sand, staking
        the human claim—

Of being alive. Of seeing the sea. The baby
        looking and looking—

And then a thing like joy, yes, did I know it? This
        open drinking in

                on her round face. As if she were seeing again
                        something novel and lost—

        I thought of the reincarnational memory
                waking up inside her.

        How some things you are happy to see again
                when you return,

                like the sea.

Mendocino 2013 / Saint Louis 2020

NOW DO YOU KNOW WHERE YOU ARE

It is another way of saying WAKE UP.

Of saying, "Get your bearings. Hear the trees."

Itself a command with a new ring of sound, here in the momentary age of Trump.

Momentary. No one lasts forever. Everything rises, hovers, and falls. "Nothing in the world beats time," you said.

You said, "The light murdered, that the truth become apparent."

I'm feeling that today, on the tenth day of the first one hundred of America's new mad king.

All of us hurtling into the year of the Fire Rooster. Which is like saying Mars × Mars. Which is to say combustible. But also the purifying fever embedded in the Greek conception of "crisis." (In a word, as you'd say, a world.)

When we met, many years ago, we talked about getting located. You were a practitioner of deep coordinates, writing from the intersection where eternal forces meet history and place. Where the soul and the body press against and into one another—so many bodies a soul has to press through: personal, familial, regional, national, global, planetary, cosmic—

"Now do you know where you are?"

I've been hearing you say that for months. You say it at three different junctures in *Deepstep Come Shining*.

Dear C.D. Wright, I don't know where I am, but you are helping me to get there.

Spirit I only met once.

January 2017

NOTES

A WALK IN THE PARK
The poem stems from thinking about the myth of Er, in Book 10 of Plato's *Republic*. Er dies, visits the afterlife, and comes back to tell the tale. He describes the Wheel of Necessity, a spindle turning the orbit "threads" of the planets. The turning spindle is the primary mover of the souls of the dead into their next bodies on earth. It is attended by the goddess Necessity in her threefold form: the Fates, who spin, measure, and cut each length of life.

I AM THAT I AM:
YHVH, as burning bush, to Moses in Exodus 3:14

No there there:
Gertrude Stein on Oakland, California (her birthplace), in *Everybody's Autobiography.*

TWO AUTUMNS, SAINT LOUIS
A Parade of Horribles:
A *parade of horribles* is a rhetorical device employing a series of progressively more terrible results following from an act. In the infamous *Dred Scott* decision, the Supreme Court resorted to a parade of horribles to describe the free movement of Black slaves if they were legally "free" in free states: a "horrible" result if the court had found in Scott's favor, which it did not. The decision became primary tinder for the coming Civil War. Parts of this "parade" appear verbatim in italics in this section of the poem.

    You can leave pennies on Dred Scott's tombstone in Calvary Cemetery in Saint Louis.

Commerce:
The italicized text beginning *John Wright* is adapted from Jeannette Cooperman, "St. Louis: A City Divided," *Al Jazeera America*, 18 August 2014:
    John Wright, former assistant superintendent of the Ferguson-

Florissant school district, remembers a chain stretched across a road to cut off access from the black city of Kinloch to then-white Ferguson. Wright is now retired and is a cultural ambassador to Senegal. "I tell people I grew up in an apartheid town," he said.

Forest Park:
I had not thought death had undone so many: Dante's *Inferno*, by way of T.S. Eliot's *The Waste Land*.

The Angel of the Spirit of the Confederacy is depicted in a thirty-two-foot granite and bronze monument presented to Forest Park in 1914 by the Daughters of the Confederacy of Saint Louis. In summer 2017, a few months after this poem was completed, the monument was finally dismantled and removed from the park.

Heroic Couplet
Material in italics is from Gregory Corso's great 1958 poem "Bomb."

Heroic Couplet, The Birth and Death Corn, and Appointment
These poems are indebted to M. Jensen, Incarnation Specialist.

Pledge
This poem is for Bailey Schaumburg.

How to Hold the Heavy Weight of Now
This poem is for Shari Lee.

For the Poets
While the speakers of most italicized quotes and references in the poem are mentioned, two are not: Rilke, whose *Duino Elegies* famously begins, in English translation, "Who, if I cried out"; and the Who, in their rock opera *Tommy*.

About Staircases

The philosopher is Gaston Bachelard. The mythographer is Joseph Campbell. The poet is Brenda Hillman. The movie referenced at the beginning of part 4 is *The Mission*.

January Garden

This poem is for G.C. Waldrep.

Now Do You Know Where You Are

The material in this piece is excerpted from "Deep Coordinates: A Letter / For C.D. Wright," composed for "School of Exactly One: C.D. Wright Memorial," a featured event at the 2017 Association of Writers and Writing Programs Conference, and later published in *Grist*.

ABOUT THE AUTHOR

Dana Levin is the author of five books of poetry. Her poems and essays have appeared in many anthologies and journals, including *Best American Poetry, The New York Times, Boston Review, The American Poetry Review, Poetry,* and *The Nation.* Her fellowships and awards include those from the National Endowment for the Arts, PEN, the Witter Bynner Foundation, and the Library of Congress, as well as the Lannan, Rona Jaffe, Whiting, and Guggenheim foundations. Levin lives in Saint Louis and currently serves as Distinguished Writer-in-Residence at Maryville University.

Lannan Literary Selections

For two decades Lannan Foundation has supported the publication and distribution of exceptional literary works. Copper Canyon Press gratefully acknowledges their support.

LANNAN LITERARY SELECTIONS 2022

Chris Abani, *Smoking the Bible*

Victoria Chang, *The Trees Witness Everything*

Nicholas Goodly, *Black Swim*

Dana Levin, *Now Do You Know Where You Are*

Michael Wasson, *Swallowed Light*

RECENT LANNAN LITERARY SELECTIONS FROM COPPER CANYON PRESS

Mark Bibbins, *13th Balloon*

Sherwin Bitsui, *Dissolve*

Jericho Brown, *The Tradition*

Victoria Chang, *Obit*

Leila Chatti, *Deluge*

Shangyang Fang, *Burying the Mountain*

June Jordan, *The Essential June Jordan*

Laura Kasischke, *Lightning Falls in Love*

Deborah Landau, *Soft Targets*

Rachel McKibbens, *blud*

Philip Metres, *Shrapnel Maps*

Aimee Nezhukumatathil, *Oceanic*

Paisley Rekdal, *Nightingale*

Natalie Scenters-Zapico, *Lima :: Limón*

Natalie Shapero, *Popular Longing*

Frank Stanford, *What About This: Collected Poems of Frank Stanford*

Arthur Sze, *The Glass Constellation: New and Collected Poems*

Fernando Valverde, *America* (translated by Carolyn Forché)

Matthew Zapruder, *Father's Day*

Poetry is vital to language and living. Since 1972, Copper Canyon Press has published extraordinary poetry from around the world to engage the imaginations and intellects of readers, writers, booksellers, librarians, teachers, students, and donors.

COPPER CANYON PRESS WISHES TO EXTEND A SPECIAL THANKS TO THE FOLLOWING SUPPORTERS WHO PROVIDED FUNDING DURING THE COVID-19 PANDEMIC:

4Culture
Academy of American Poets (Literary Relief Fund)
City of Seattle Office of Arts & Culture
Community of Literary Magazines and Presses (Literary Relief Fund)
Economic Development Council of Jefferson County
National Book Foundation (Literary Relief Fund)
Poetry Foundation
U.S. Department of the Treasury Payroll Protection Program

WE ARE GRATEFUL FOR THE MAJOR SUPPORT PROVIDED BY:

TO LEARN MORE ABOUT UNDERWRITING
COPPER CANYON PRESS TITLES,
PLEASE CALL 360-385-4925 EXT. 103

WE ARE GRATEFUL FOR THE MAJOR SUPPORT PROVIDED BY:

Anonymous (3)

Jill Baker and Jeffrey Bishop

Anne and Geoffrey Barker

In honor of Ida Bauer, Betsy
    Gifford, and Beverly Sachar

Donna Bellew

Matthew Bellew

Sarah Bird

Will Blythe

John Branch

Diana Broze

John R. Cahill

Sarah Cavanaugh

Stephanie Ellis-Smith and Douglas
    Smith

Austin Evans

Saramel Evans

Mimi Gardner Gates

Gull Industries Inc. on behalf of
    William True

The Trust of Warren A. Gummow

William R. Hearst, III

Carolyn and Robert Hedin

Bruce Kahn

Phil Kovacevich and Eric Wechsler

Lakeside Industries Inc. on behalf
    of Jeanne Marie Lee

Maureen Lee and Mark Busto

Peter Lewis and Johnna Turiano

Ellie Mathews and Carl Youngmann
    as The North Press

Larry Mawby and Lois Bahle

Hank and Liesel Meijer

Jack Nicholson

Gregg Orr

Petunia Charitable Fund and
    adviser Elizabeth Hebert

Suzanne Rapp and Mark Hamilton

Adam and Lynn Rauch

Emily and Dan Raymond

Joseph C. Roberts

Jill and Bill Ruckelshaus

Cynthia Sears

Kim and Jeff Seely

Joan F. Woods

Barbara and Charles Wright

Caleb Young as C. Young Creative

The dedicated interns and
    faithful volunteers of
    Copper Canyon Press

The Chinese character for poetry is made up
of two parts: "word" and "temple."
It also serves as pressmark for
Copper Canyon Press.

This book is set in ITC Galliard Pro
Book design by Gopa & Ted2, Inc.
Printed on archival-quality paper.